SIGNED
16.03.99

Dungeness – a unique place
Copyright © Ged Robinson 1998

All Rights Reserved

No part of this book may be reproduced in any form by photocopying or by any electronic or mechanical means, including information storage or retrieval systems, without the permission in writing from both the copyright owner and the publisher of this book.

ISBN 0 9535022 0 1

First published in December 1998
by Sutton House, Iford, East Sussex, BN7 3EU
01273 476847

Printed in Great Britain

Dungeness – a unique place

Contents

Introduction – Ged Robinson 1
Memories – Ken Oiller 2
The Natural Landscape – Mariana Hollis 3
Memories – Ken Oiller 16
Nuclear Power – Dungeness "A" and "B" – Ginny Smith 17
Memories – Ken Oiller 26
The Fishing Community: Voices of the Wives – Ged Robinson 27
Memories – Ken Oiller 44
Artists at Dungeness – Keith Clements 46
Memories – Ken Oiller 57
Conservation and Wildlife – Simon Busuttil 59
Conclusion – Ken Oiller. 68
The Contributors 69
Acknowledgements 71
Bibliography 72

**Cover Photograph "Baxters" – wooden overshoes used to walk on the shingle
(see page 31)** (Photographer, David Smith)

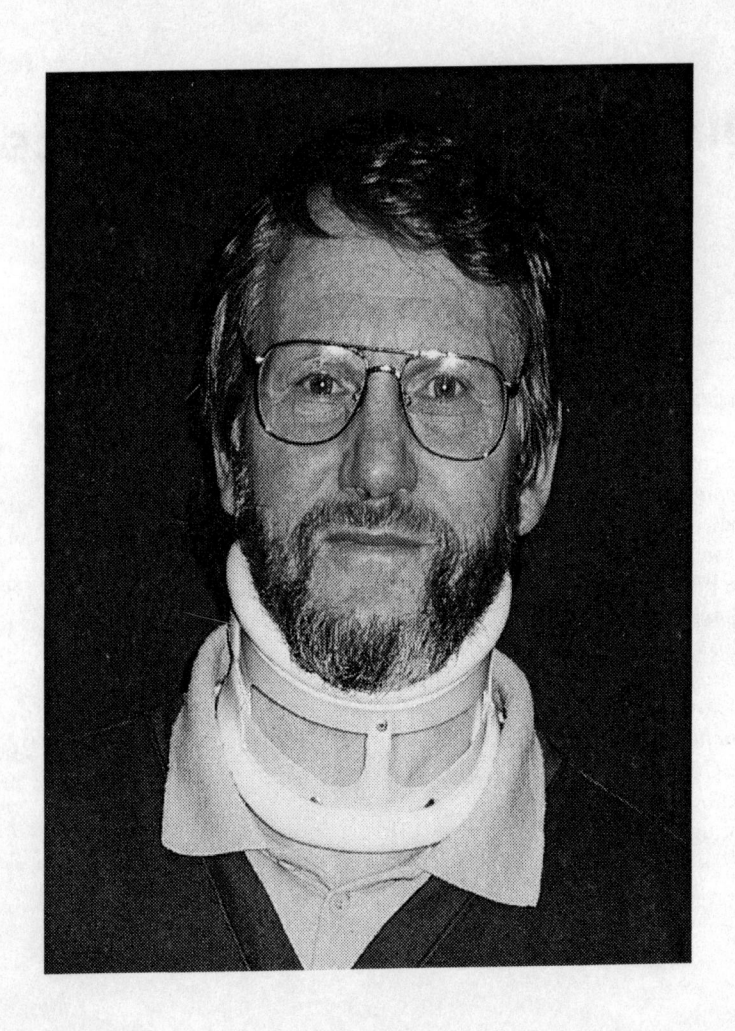

Ken Oiller
Photographer, David Smith

Introduction – Ged Robinson

"Dungeness is a unique place, of that there is no doubt." In one succinct sentence a resident fisherman, Ken Oiller, conveys the essence of Dungeness. This bleak, wild, wind-swept peninsula, a true twentieth century wilderness has attracted naturalists, ornithologists, writers, poets, painters, photographers, anglers and holidaymakers. It has also had to withstand the intrusion of a nuclear power station and to accept the more recent invasion of tourists and the media. Behind these activities, but increasingly less visible, stands the fishing community – a continuous line of the same four families living and fishing on Dungeness beach for almost two centuries.

This book is an attempt to co-ordinate these disparate histories, communities and organisations so that, for the first time, Dungeness – this *"unique place"* can be viewed and understood in its entirety.

I was born at Pleasant Cottage, just two properties along from where I now live. My father, John Oiller, was a member of one of the fishing families living in this area for generations.

One of my earliest memories, at around age three, is of being taken to our local public house, The Britannia. I showed off my amazing memory by reciting the names of fifty-two cricketers that I had on a set of cigarette cards, as my father held them up one by one.

Dungeness School, which I attended from 1937, was about half a mile away. When I was 5 years and a few days old, my mother considered I could walk to school on my own. I set out, but had only gone about 100 yards when I came across a grass snake. Having been warned not to touch any snakes in case they were vipers, I turned back, terrified and ran home shouting "It's a wiper, it's a wiper! – my Vs and Ws were a bit mixed up in those days.

Our teacher, Miss Bottle, used to take us on nature walks across the shingle to Denge Marsh. During the summer we were allowed to play in an area of tall reeds. We would join the tops of a patch of reeds and hollow out the centre to create wigwams. These years were some of the happiest of my life.

My best friend and closest companion in those early years was Bob Tart, from Ferndale Cottage. It was his father, Punch, who taught me to swim. One lovely summer's day we were on the beach and Punch was giving us rides behind a rowing boat. We were wearing swimming costumes and holding on to the back of the boat whilst he rowed, towing us along behind. The other lads were letting go of the boat and swimming to the shore about 20 yards away. When it came to my turn to let go I said "I can't swim". "What," said Punch, "a fisherman's son who can't swim? We can't have that." He reached out and rapped my knuckles hard, making me lose my grip. I swam to the beach with some strange and suddenly invented stroke. When I had regained my breath, I thought, "I can swim", and immediately ran back into the sea.

Ken Oiller

The Natural Landscape – Mariana Hollis

Dungeness in Kent is at the apex of an inverted triangle with a curving base line from Rye in the west, through Hamstreet to Hythe in the east. The 'Ness' is the area of shingle ridges, which form a nose-shaped incursion to the sea from Lydd and Romney Marsh. From the land, Dungeness can only be approached across marshes. Scenically and geologically the two are intimately linked. It is the combination of this and the sea, which conveys such a sense of space: an abrupt and remarkable scenic change from the well wooded, rolling, intensively farmed countryside to the North.

Visitors become familiar with the nature of this surrounding countryside, from the twisting roads which approach the area, from Folkestone, Ashford, Tenterden and Rye. A steep and irregular hilly incline marks the ancient coastline. The Royal Military Canal follows the transition from rolling to flat land, from enclosed to open, from arable to pastoral, from density of population, habitation and vegetation, to sparsity. The flatness of the marshland has the unnatural feel of all reclaimed land. Yet, as the marsh is traversed and the low sweeps of the Dungeness shingle ridges come into view, it becomes obvious that the natural agency of the sea is as much at work here as man's efforts to keep the sea at bay.

Historical Background
The marshes have been reclaimed from the sea over the last 1,000 years. It has been a gradual transition, which was accelerated when the economic potential of Romney Marsh for raising sheep was fully realised. Before their reclamation the marshlands were tidal flats and creeks through which the River Rother flowed to the sea. The position of the river mouth was to change markedly even within historic time. This was as a result of changing shingle-spit

THE CHANGING FACE OF DUNGENESS
A. 5,000 to 3,000 YEARS AGO

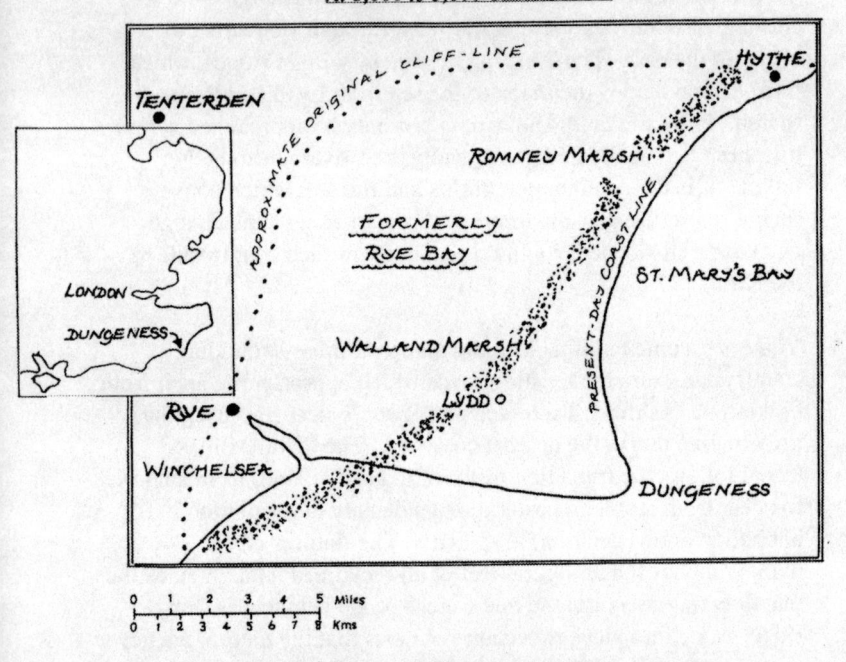

SANDY BAR ENCLOSES RYE BAY

Waves bring shingle and sand from the south-west and gradually build up a barrier beach across the bay, creating a lagoon.
As the lagoon silts up, so trees grow and woodland develops in the west, leading to accumulation of peat. The River Rother crosses this area of peat and trees to flow through salt marsh and tidal mud-flats to reach the sea near Hythe in the north. Meanwhile at the west end of the bay, the coastline near Winchelsea is changing as waves start to build out shingle ridges from the barrier beach. These will eventually, (over a 4,000 year period,) form the 'nose' of Dungeness.

There is evidence of early settlement from 3,800 years ago near Lydd.
Bronze low flanged axes were retrieved from the Pioneer gravel pit nearby.
It is possible that Lydd was a landing point for cross-channel trade.
There was also very early development of the salt extraction industry from the tidal mud-flats behind Lydd.

formation, the influence of continual wave action and the occasional dramatic storm.

Romney Marsh was once Romney (or Rye) Bay. About 5,000 years ago a sandy bar gradually developed across the bay, changing it to an enclosed lagoon (see Diagram A). The sandy bar was sufficiently stable to support early settlement in the area near Lydd 3,700 years ago. With the sea on one side of this settlement and the lagoon on the other, there was potential for fishing, and later for salt extraction from tidal salt marshes and possibly some early coastal trade to develop.

The new coastline and the area enclosed by the bar continued to change. Instead of a bay, the coast was now 'straighter'. It seems likely that this change initiated a different form of shingle accumulation. Shingle ridges started to form a triangular shaped headland or 'ness' further into the sea from Rye and Winchelsea area. These early ridges date back about 3,000 years. This was the start of the complex formation of shingle ridges which is Dungeness today.

Within the last 2,000 years, changes have occurred which are still recognisable in the landscape. In 275 A.D. the Romans built a defensive, coastal fort at Portus Lemanis on the hillside below Lympe. The remains are still evident at Stutfall Castle. We are also indebted to the Romans for the embankment known as the Rhee Wall, which enclosed much of the northern part of Romney Marsh. By 1086 A.D. and the Domesday Book, the scattered churches recorded in this part of the marsh indicate that this was well-established dry land (see Diagram B). Despite climatic setbacks, reclamation was also progressing to the south of the Rhee Wall although there was little occupation of this part of the marsh. There is no clear written evidence of reclamation work prior to the

B. PRE-ROMAN TIMES to THE DOMESDAY BOOK

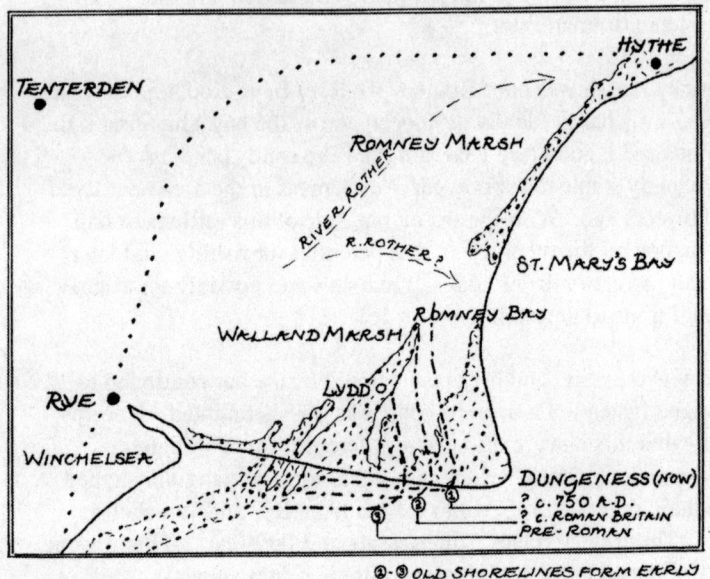

FORMATION OF SHINGLE RIDGES

After the initial formation of the sandy bar across Rye Bay, the overiding factor in the coastal development of this area was the movement of shingle eastwards, by 'Longshore Drift'. South-westerly winds brought waves carrying flint pebbles from the nearest chalk outcrops, until they piled up, ridge after ridge, east of Rye and Winchelsea. Shingle ridges, thrown up initially by storm action, built up into complex spits and barriers as shown on the plan above.

Man was also starting to influence shoreline development. In 275 A.D. the Romans built a vast fort at Portus Lemanis below Lympne as a defensive post against Saxon pirates.(The ruins are still there today) As the reclamation of coastal marshlands proceeded and sea defences were strengthened, so changes occurred in the former lagoon. By the Domesday Book, 1086, the Rother had broken through the shingle bar and reached the sea near Romney. Records of scattered churches show that the north of Romney Marsh had already dried out. The headland of Dungeness continued to grow out into the sea and Denge Marsh became dry land.

twelfth century, but it had almost certainly begun long before that.

In 1287 A.D. violent storms caused considerable change. The mouth of the river Rother, which was first near Hythe, then at Romney, now opened to the sea near Rye. The harbour of Romney was destroyed and blocked by shingle. Old Winchelsea and Broomhill were destroyed and abandoned and the shingle barrier at Rye was washed away. Since 1287, the history of coastal changes and reclamation of the marshland is fairly well known from contemporary documents and maps. During this time the influence of man has been greatest, both in building coastal defences and harbour works and in reclamation. For example, the successive works to keep Rye Harbour open have contributed largely to the retention of shingle west of the harbour and the depletion of shingle to the east at Camber and at Broomhill. In Romney Marsh itself, the reclamations appear to have progressed from east to west. To the west most of the area as far as East Guldefors was reclaimed between the twelfth and seventeenth centuries. The valleys of the Rother, Brede and Tillingham have been reclaimed in more modern times but are still partly tidal. Denge Marsh and neighbouring areas in the headland had dried out by 1287. Open freshwater pits were forming in the shingle. These pits are now over a mile from the sea.

The area of shingle itself continued to grow to such an extent that it became a danger to shipping, not only from the shallow water but also from the enticement of 'Wreckers' using fires and flares to lure in the ships. To offset the danger the first coal-fired wooden lighthouse was built in 1615. The rapidity with which the location of lighthouses at Dungeness had to change, charts the rapidity with which the shingle headland was growing. By 1635 a second lighthouse was necessary. In 1792 a third was built 500 yards seawards from the first. In 1904 came the fourth lighthouse. The most recent one was built forward of this in 1961, because the building of the nuclear power station had partially obliterated the 1904 light (see Diagram C). Coastal change is still taking place, although the processes at work are changing. For example, the building of the power station has made continuous shingle stabilisation essential in its immediate environs. This will become even more crucial if the predicted rise in sea level takes place - could this mean a return from Romney Marsh to Romney Bay?

Shingle
It is the shingle itself, which makes Dungeness so distinctive. The landsurface of the Dungeness foreland is entirely shingle, covering an area of 72 square kilometres, (12kms by 6kms). The shingle is up to 17 metres thick in places. It is the largest surface area of shingle in Europe. Only 1/3 of the surface is vegetated, the rest is exposed continually to the elements. The virtually soil-free nature of Dungeness is in sharp contrast to the fertile alluvial soils of the reclaimed marshland.

The shingle consists almost entirely of rounded flint pebbles ranging in size from pea gravel to medium cobbles. Their composition is 98% flint and 2% quartzite and sandstone. The shingle has been transported from the chalk downs of Sussex, Hampshire and Dorset. The chalk there was formed in marine conditions 90 million years ago and covered much of southern England. Then, 2-3 million years ago, during the last Ice Age, much of the soft chalk was weathered away. The harder flints were washed down to the Channel beaches as the sea level gradually rose with the melting of the ice. Southwesterly winds and wave action along the south coast caused the shingle to pile up in vast quantities at Dungeness, as part of a marine process known as long shore drift. By this process, a wave strikes the shore at an angle carrying pebbles up the beach with it. The water then runs down the beach again and carries the pebbles back. The next wave picks

C. PRESENT DAY DUNGENESS

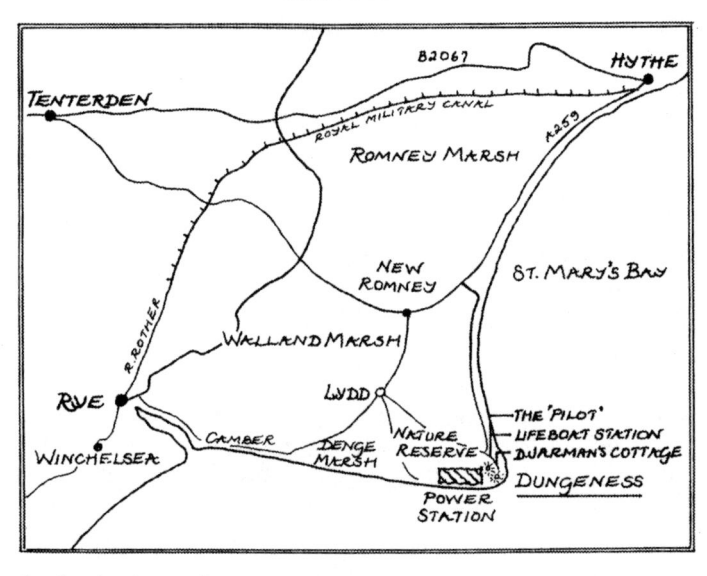

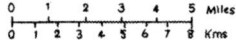

Map showing present-day Dungeness area with locations including Tenterden, Hythe, Romney Marsh, New Romney, St. Mary's Bay, Rye, Winchelsea, Walland Marsh, Lydd, Camber, Denge Marsh, Nature Reserve, The 'Pilot', Lifeboat Station, Dungeon Cottage, Dungeness, and Power Station. Scale: 0–5 Miles / 0–8 Kms. Features labelled include B2067, Royal Military Canal, A259, and R. Rother.

THE GREAT STORMS OF THE THIRTEENTH CENTURY AND AFTER

In 1287 A.D. violent storms wrought considerable change to the coastline and the drainage pattern. The mouth of the Rother was diverted to Rye. Old Winchelsea and Broomhill were destroyed. The storms resulted in the formation of the Open Pits which an important present-day ecological feature of the shingle headland and now, over a mile from the sea.

Reclamation continued after the storms and defensive sea walls were built. The marshland was to become renowned as a sheep raising area.
The shingle headland continued to grow outward and became a danger to shipping. As a result the first lighthouse was built in 1615.
By 1792 further shingle had accummulated and a new lighthouse was built 500 yards seawards from the first. Since that time two further lighthouses have been built to mark the changing coastline.
Since 1965 nuclear power has been generated at Dungeness. Shingle accummulation is now carefully monitored. The shingle provides a particular habitat for a wide range of flora and fauna. Some areas of shingle and its associated vegetation are now protected in a National Nature Reserve

up the pebbles and transports them further along the beach by the same method.

The supply of shingle along the coast continued to grow. The prevailing eastward long shore drift led to a spit and headland formation known as a cuspate foreland. The geology of this was first researched extensively by Lewis in 1932. His interpretation of the foreland was that new ridges were being partly built from the destruction of older ridges. Also, that the easterly ridges were the most recent. This is still the case, but there is much recent modification.

Every year, during the winter months, more than 100,000 cubic metres of shingle is moved naturally eastwards around Dungeness Point by long shore drift. The cumulative effect of this on the development of the headland is not as it once was, because now the shingle is moved by lorry from the east shore, back to the southern shore to protect the power station. Even so, the eastern shore is still growing outwards slowly whilst the southern shore is losing ground. The way in which the shingle ridges swirl in a crescent fashion around the headland can be seen by eye from the lighthouse.

Shingle Vegetation
For well-adapted shingle loving plants the shingle ridge formation at Dungeness is an unusually extensive habitat. Microhabitats for plants are also formed by the climatic and geological differences between the exposed tops of the mature ridges or 'fulls', where there are smaller stones and the more sheltered troughs or 'lows', where the stones are coarser in texture.

At first, the most obvious question seems to be, how did any vegetation become established? Initially no soil was present and the shingle was constantly exposed to salt laden winds straight off the sea. Very few plants, save a few lichens, could survive under such conditions. It was the lichens *(Cladonia species)*, however, that were to form the basis for all future plant growth here. As the lichens develop on the stones themselves, so they accumulate some organic material as a basis for other plants to establish. Through the succession of lichen growth and decay, conditions are gradually formed that are suitable for more sophisticated maritime plants.

The first plant to become established on dry shingle is Sea Kale, *(Crambe maritima)*. Great swathes of this attractive plant are present immediately behind the shoreline at Dungeness. It has penetrating water-seeking roots, which also help to stabilise the plant in the face of strong wind. The coarse leaves of the Crambe resist dehydration whilst absorbing all available moisture. It is therefore, an excellent colonising plant although the leaves are vulnerable to trampling. In the autumn the large seed heads are frequently seen blowing across the beaches. When they die down in situ they provide additional organic matter and nutrients for growth.

Once the Sea Kale is firmly established on the outer (seaward) shingle ridges, the conditions improve a little for other plants. The availability of non-saline fresh water is of prime importance. Plants colonising the bare shingle depend on the water retaining effect of the stones as a mulch, to hold rainwater and dew in the upper layers of the shingle. Sea Campion *(Silene vulgaris maritima)* would associate with the Sea Kale on the outer ridges. Progressing landwards, Curled Dock *(Rumex crispus)* and Common Sorrel *(Rumex acetosa)* would be the next to find the marginally improved conditions suitable. Slightly further inland, False Oat Grass *(Arrhenatherum elatius)* and Sweet Vernal Grass *(Anthoxanthum odoratum)* are found on the ridges.

Despite colonisation by these plants, very little soil development takes place on the outer (seaward) shingle ridges. Even so, a present day feature of the outer ridges is the cultivation of remarkable gardens associated with the dwellings along the shore road. The film director Derek Jarman was responsible for the most famous of these. Around his house, naturally occurring species are combined with plants that can tolerate the conditions. The planting has then been artistically embellished with mainly natural and local artefacts.

The Power Station from Dungeness RSPB Reserve
Photograph courtesy of the RSPB

The general impression of the Dungeness coastal strip is of a sparse and barren landscape. Yet away from the shore road the vegetation cover starts to thicken. The older and more sheltered inland ridges can support the growth of Broom *(Cytisus scoparius)*. Broom plays a vital part in encouraging further vegetation cover.

As Broom grows the tips of each shoot are extended. Gradually, over a 15 to 20 year period, the middle of the plant dies down. A sheltered central core is left. This is filled with decaying organic matter, an ideal venue for the establishment of more specialised plants. These include the English Stonecrop *(Sedum anglicum)*, the Nottingham Catchfly *(Silene nutans)*, Sheep's Bit *(Jasione montana)* and Sheep's Sorrel *(Rumex acetisella)*. As a result of the establishment of the Broom there is a higher level of humus in the soil, vegetation cover is more or less continuous and the diversity of species increases.

A very specific succession of plants has therefore been responsible for the vegetation cover we see today. There are also particular plants – Ragwort *(Senecio sp)*, the Yellow Horned Poppy *(Glaucium flavum)*, Vipers Bugloss *(Echinen vulgare)*, Red Valerian *(Ceotranthus ruber)*, Gorse *(Ulex europaens)* and Bramble *(Rubus sp)* – characteristic of the ground that has been disturbed by gravel extraction, leisure activities and other general "damage" to the naturally vegetated ridges.

As a result of gravel extraction there is also very much more open water at Dungeness than naturally occurs there. A very small proportion of the areas of open water is natural wetlands, yet these have the greatest ecological significance. The largest of the wetlands are the 'Open Pits' which are now part of the Dungeness RSPB Nature Reserve. Over 700 years ago there was salt water in them. It is now fresh. As the headland of Dungeness continued to grow, rainwater and water percolation had more significance than the sea. Today the pits form one of the largest areas of freshwater on shingle in Europe. They did support a unique sedge-rich marshland, but are now overtaken by Salix. Since the 1970s the water table has been lowered by water abstraction and hydrological changes associated with gravel extraction. This has increased the tendency for the pits to silt up with a greater development of reed swamp and shrubby willows *(sallow carr).*

The shingle and the coastal proximity of the Dungeness foreland make it a challenging site for the establishment of plants. Those that do survive here are specifically adapted to the harsh conditions. With some varieties, such as the Sea Kale, this means there are unusually extensive areas of a relatively uncommon plant. It has become a particularly characteristic aspect of the foreshore landscape at Dungeness and is in evidence throughout the year, as winter greenery, scented summer flowers or the large wind-blown seedheads of autumn.

The Power Station with Natural Vegetation
Photograph courtesy of the RSPB

Most of the species occurring here naturally, are very vulnerable to change, the Sea Kale included. Changes to the natural alignment of the shingle, development, gravel extraction and water table fluctuations, all result in change to the natural vegetation. Harm can also come more directly, through trampling, by machinery and by foot. There is now special legal protection to the most fragile shingle habitats, through their designation as a Site of Special Scientific Interest (SSSI). The National Nature Reserve status of part of the area brings with it a commitment to positive action for protection. The protected sites are small in relation to Dungeness as a whole, whilst the scale of the enterprises that take place there are vast. The protection of the nuclear power station alone, annually causes redistribution of great quantities of shoreline shingle.

Dungeness is a dynamic landscape. The constant changes make it uniquely interesting and in the future, there could be changes on at least as great a scale as there have been in the recent past.

*****

In around 1937 the SS Ansversville was grounded. I recall my brother Eric calling "come out and look, there's a ship ashore". When I looked out, I saw a huge liner "parked" next to the lifeboat station. Fortunately, the ship had grounded while the tide was still rising and so at high tide she was able to refloat herself and so no great damage was done.

Once a huge cask of sherry was washed ashore about 200 yards from our cottage. It was the duty of the local inhabitants to inform the Customs Officers of any such valuable items, but this was too good an opportunity to miss. I can still see my father trudging across the shingle with two pails hanging from the yokes across his shoulders.

Anything that was delivered up by the sea and was usable was considered a bonus to the fishermen that made a hard earned living here. When chests of tea were washed ashore on the point and along the western beach, my brother and I dragged our little sledge, made from a box with barrel staves fixed to the bottom, along the beach. We filled it with tealeaves and took it home to Mum.

Three houses along from where we lived was a cottage with a tower built beside it. George Bates, who lived there, was a shipping agent for Lloyds of London. His job was to call up the ships that passed Dungeness by using an Aldis Lamp and morse code. Then he phoned Lloyds with the name and expected time of arrival of the ship. The pilot cutter used to lay off Dungeness and Mr Bates would take pilots out in his small boat to put aboard the ships that were bound for London, or to bring them ashore to catch the train to Gravesend if the ship was on its outward journey.

Ken Oiller

Nuclear Power – Dungeness "A" and "B" – Ginny Smith

Approaching Dungeness on the coastal road across the marshes from the west, the landscape is one great expanse of sky and flat fields stretching into the distance dotted with sheep and the occasional surprising and incongruous group of swans waddling alongside a roadside dyke. Into this rather untidy rural scene march two lines of gigantic pylons, crossing river and road, converging at a point on the horizon where the outline of three great industrial towers dwarf the pinnacles of Lydd church tower.

The nuclear power stations impinge upon the landscape in surprising ways: inside one of the wooden cottages they appear unexpectedly, framed in a window; when you think you are walking away from them, the reactor towers are there ahead of you. Dungeness has become synonymous with the three great towers and the lines of pylons stretching away from them. In people's awareness they have taken over what was there before. When they think of Dungeness they think not of the unique peninsular or of the community that is based there, but of the nuclear power stations. What exists now and what existed before the power stations is in danger of being forgotten.

The first power station was born in the early 1960s out of a forgetting and a denial of much that was unique about the place and the people of Dungeness. It was the product of government and scientific enthusiasm for what was seen as the cleanliness and efficiency of nuclear energy and the surge of nuclear power station building in the 50s and 60s. Sites that offered access to deep water, reasonable communication but were away from major population centres, were targeted. Almost by definition these included some of the wildest most unique and beautiful spots in the country. The weight of support for nuclear power in government circles created an impetus that was difficult to resist, and public concern for the environment scarcely existed in the 1950s. Opposing the construction of a particular power station was, therefore, difficult and unlikely to be successful. The overwhelming imperative was seen to be the national requirement for more energy, produced cleanly and efficiently.

The Dungeness power station project was veiled in secrecy. James Adams, Planning Officer for Kent County Council in 1957 first became aware of a possible proposal to build a nuclear power station on Dungeness through a press report describing *"secret borings"* near Lydd. Wimpey, the construction firm, whose trucks appeared on the site the following year, responded to enquiries with a stern rebuff – *"The subject is a closed book. Nothing can be said."* Other sites in the SouthEast were being investigated at the same time, including the outstandingly beautiful Cuckmere Haven in Sussex, Kingsnorth in Kent and the Isle of Sheppey. The alternative Kent sites were rejected as being too close to centres of population and, in one case, as being a Site of Special Scientific Interest. Cuckmere presented problems because of, apparently the proximity of the town of Seaford. The assumption underlying these arguments would seem to point to Dungeness attracting few, if any, of these objections. It was almost as if the little town of Lydd, the village of Greatstone, let alone the community on Dungeness itself did not exist. The knowledge of the vagaries of the sea, the constantly shifting shingle, the shared wisdom that existed within the community of fishermen and their families were entirely passed over.

Dungeness "A", a Magnox twin reactor station was built in spite of objections from Kent County Council, the National Farmers Union, the Fishermen's Protection Association and the Nature Conservancy Council.

The construction of the power station changed the nature of the landscape and the lives of the people living and working off the gravel peninsular. The freedom of residents to cross the shingle was considerably curtailed by the perimeter fences around the building site and the access road.

"But the worst thing about it was the constant pounding of the pile-drivers and the awful fusty smell in the air. If you dig really deep into the beach you get a musty sort of smell."

The power station came on stream in 1965 and had cost over £60 million.

Dungeness "A" Nuclear Power Station
Photographer, David Smith

Over the years officialdom has frequently failed to consult the residents of Dungeness, to respect their expertise and to recognise their fierce pride in their community. Some love the sight of the power station all lit up at night, but have a huge sense of frustration when it continues to be lit up during local power cuts! They cannot understand why the power station was built on a site where two old wooden houses were disappearing into the sea because of the shifting shingle.

The community has felt invisible. A fisherman attending a liaison meeting found that the plans did not show the cottage where his parents lived and a report on the site mentioned only a *"small gathering of holiday chalets"*! A club was set up for the power station employees on the outskirts of Lydd and took the name Dungeness Sports and Social Club – but the people of Dungeness have never been included – *"It was a power station club, not a Dungeness one."*

Erosion and shifting shingle was a problem from the start. The Central Electricity Generating Board (CEGB) planners had consulted records going back 150 years when they considered the site. They had also brought in consultants who assured them that *"The minor erosion processes would become stable over a long term period"*. The local fishermen knew better. They knew that every ten years they have to dig out their winch anchors and move them nearer to the sea on the east of the Point, where tons of shingle from the west are dumped by the action of the tides.

The key concern of the fishermen throughout the building and commissioning of both the "A" and "B" stations was the impact of the cooling inlet pipes on their fishing territory and the catch and the changing pattern of erosion that the transport of shingle from one side of the spit to the other might be causing. The concrete slipway down which the Dungeness Lifeboat was launched had been undermined by erosion. A large public meeting was held and a new one was constructed further up the beach with contributions from the CEGB.

From the start of the Dungeness "A" project there were rumours of gigantic fish being seen around the outlet pipes which pumped thousands of gallons of hot water into the sea. Experts were reputed to have found large sharks, squids and jellyfish in the vicinity of nuclear power stations around the coast of Britain. Recently, Kent Police are said to have received a report of Vietnamese restaurant owners setting out in rubber dinghies to fish the waters around the power station for giant prawns!

The inlet pipes also caused concern. A report in the Kent Messenger in March 1964 quoted fisheries officers as having estimated that 15 stone of fish a day were being sucked into the water intakes, many of them small and immature fish that should have been providing the breeding stocks for future catches. Kent Fisheries Officer, Mr Richardson said he did not know if there was any truth in the stories about workmen getting fish out of the inlet pipes and taking them home to eat!

Headlines in the Kentish Express 10 years later reflected a problem that had on a number of occasions brought the power station to a halt – *"Shivery Sprats in Nuclear Blackout."* A shoal of cold sprats, looking for a warm refuge in the icy English Channel, swam into the power station's cooling water intake causing the collapse of a sea water filter and clogging the cooling system. Local fishermen had warned them to run the pipes further seaward as the intakes were placed exactly where the sprats naturally shoaled.

The power station could have been sited 300 yards inland, but this would have required an extension of the cooling pipe. The consequences are that in the winter period 300 tons of shingle a day have to be moved from one side of the point to the other by lorry to prevent the power station being washed out to sea.

Some of the residents' other concerns about the impact of such a vast construction site a few hundred yards from their doors have happily not been realised. An army of building workers living within the perimeter fence caused few problems to Dungeness residents. Many drank in the local pubs the Pilot and the Britannia. Sometimes they didn't make it home and were found asleep on the shingle.

The power station supplied a useful alternative source of employment during construction, but the nature of the work has changed with the commissioning of both "A" and "B". Now many of the jobs on site demand a sophisticated level of skill and technical knowledge. People who were attracted to the area twenty or thirty years ago by the high level of demand for unskilled labour have now been laid off and are unable to find alternative work locally. This has lead to pockets of unemployment and social problems.

These incomers stayed longer than might have originally been predicted. When Dungeness "A" was nearing completion rumours began about the building of a second power station, which would occupy the remainder of the site. Once again the origins of the project were shrouded in secrecy. Very little was known even in the House of Commons about the Powell Committee, whose remit was to report on the future of Britain's atom-power programme. In 1964 the Folkestone Herald reported an application by the CEGB to Kent County Council and the then Ministry of Power to build a second power station. It was hoped the power station would come into operation in 1970 and make the two stations combined, one of the biggest nuclear power generating facilities in the world. A spokesman for the CEGB said that the land at Dungeness had in fact been earmarked for such a use when plans were drawn up for the first station, *"because of the natural advantages of Dungeness for nuclear generation, particularly the outstanding sea-water cooling facilities"*. It was decided that the second power station would be of the Advanced Gas Cooled Reactor type.

Dungeness "B" – known as Blunderess "B" – was finally commissioned ten years after its planned start-up date, following a seemingly never-ending series of accidents and design or construction faults.

Power Station from RSPB Visitor Centre
Photograph courtesy of the RSPB

As the new building was contained within the existing site and its construction followed almost directly on from the "A" station the decision to build had little impact on the residents of Dungeness. However, the constant stream of reports about the discovery of design faults, defects in operating systems and accidents on site started to raise concerns about safety and noise pollution. The regular release of pressure through the steam valves could be heard as far away as Greatstone and one resident of Dungeness described the noise in her cottage as terrifying. At times the ground vibrates and on one occasion anglers who had been peacefully dosing beside their rods at the edge of the beach were seen *"running like rabbits across the shingle"*.

The CEGB became more aware of the concerns about safety and in the late 70s drew up an emergency plan for nuclear power stations, copies of which were lodged with New Romney and Folkestone Councils and were available in the local libraries. Every resident is now issued annually with a calendar containing detailed instructions about evacuation procedures and what to do in the event of an accident.

When Magnox Electric and Nuclear Electric took over the running of the two power stations in the 1980s, more attention was given to safety procedures and a mock evacuation was staged. Residents found it difficult to take the exercise seriously when bus loads of "evacuees" were taken to the wrong assembly point, the supply of sweets – iodine tablets to counteract the effects of radiation – was exhausted and an elderly lady who volunteered to take part was turned away because she was not sufficiently mobile! They were also concerned that one of the emergency assembly points was at the visitors Centre at the power station – *"the last thing we will want to do in an emergency is walk towards the power station"*.

When it began to emerge that a site was being prospected for a new power station, opposition grew. Some of the cottages would be only 150 yards from the perimeter fence and The Pilot pub would have been overshadowed by the building. A wide range of interest groups united to fight any proposal to build a third power station on Dungeness, joined by the Dungeness Leaseholders Association and a group of residents whose acronym was memorably "SODOFF" – Save Our Dungeness Official Fighting Force.

Argument rumbled on for many months and the proposal finally foundered not as a result of local opposition, but after the discovery of a suspected seismic fault running directly below the proposed site.

The residents' relationship with the great bulk of their near neighbour has matured and settled down over the years with greater openness and goodwill being displayed on the part of the organisations now running the power stations. Local liaison committees have been established for a decade or more and residents, staff and managers exchange friendly greetings when their paths cross.

One evening a mother and daughter crept out to hang a large "Happy Birthday" banner on the perimeter fence to surprise the daughter's husband the following day when he arrived for work. With memories of nuclear power protesters attaching teddy bears to the fence and wielding wire clippers, the station manager was calling the security guards when he recognised the perpetrators. When the surprise was explained, he roared with laughter and the banner remained in place ...

... as do the power stations, although they will be entering a different phase of their existence. Dungeness "A" has already been granted an extension to its operating life, but is likely to close soon after the millennium. Dungeness "B" is due to be decommissioned in 2010. The bulk of the structures will remain in place until someone somewhere discovers what to do about the currently insoluble problem of disposing of defunct nuclear power stations. So, the huge structures with their potential problems continue to overshadow the lives of the people of Dungeness: *"It's not that we're anti-nuclear, it's that they have taken away our identity."*

*****

In the early years of my life here, many of the fishing families kept goats for milking. My mother always kept two or three which were allowed to wander freely on the beach. There was fairly good scrub and rough grazing for them to the landward side of the cottages.

One of my mother's goats was called Elizabeth and used to take umbrage if you shouted the word "rhubarb" at her. If she was grazing lose near the house we would hide round a corner and then pop our heads out and shout the magic word at her. She immediately charged, head down towards us. We would run back round the corner and up the steps to the net-loft. We played this game for an hour or more at a time. Each time she responded in the same way. Great fun for us, but I don't know what effect it had on the milk yield.

Our purpose built wooden dwellings had none of the modern conveniences that we all take for granted today. All the water had to be carried to the homes in pails slung on wooden yokes carried across the shoulders. The hand pump was situated about thirty yards on the inland side of our cottage and as soon as they were big enough every child was expected to take their turn in pumping up and carrying the water to the house. There was no electricity and all the cooking was done on a big black range.

Bath nights were also a difficult problem. First of all mother would fill the large wood fired copper in the kitchen to heat the water. The boys took turns to take a bath in a long metal "bungalow" bath in front of the living room fire. We were sent up to bed when it was our sisters' turn, but we had discovered that if we left the door open a little and angled the bedside mirror just right, we could have a perfect view. We had learned a lot about the formation of the female body before our trick was discovered. The door was firmly locked after that!

Charlie Mannering the greengrocer came from Lydd once a week on his horse and cart loaded with vegetables – not much fruit, as we couldn't afford it in those days. As children we also looked forward to the weekly visit by the grocer's van from Whites Stores – the only day of the week we would have bought cake and perhaps a few sweets.

Ken Oiller

The Fishing Community: Voices of the Wives – Ged Robinson

As a visitor it is difficult to "read" the buildings at Dungeness. The lifeboat station, the lighthouse, the light railway, the two pubs and the tearoom are open to visitors but the small buildings that are randomly scattered over the shingle remain an enigma. We can only view their exteriors and nowhere is there information available on the origins of this community - it lies locked in the memories of the residents themselves. Dungeness is seen by many only through the poetic eye of Derek Jarman. Here, five fishermen's wives give us a colourful insight into the cultural history of Dungeness.

Doris Tart, born in 1921 at Dungeness, at her present home, is justly proud of her lineage as she stems from two longstanding Dungeness fishing families, the Tarts and the Oillers, a favourite quote being: *"my mother was a Tart that married an Oiller and I was an Oiller that married a Tart"*.

The Tarts (originally Tarte, Doris' maternal grandfather had been Isaac Bongaurde Tarte), were Huguenots escaping from France, arriving at Dungeness in the early 1800s, whilst the Oillers were a fishing family from Cornwall that came to Dungeness in the mid-nineteenth century.

Photographer, David Smith

Pauline Fair, born in 1943, also has connections with the Tart family. Although originating from Kennington near Ashford in Kent, aged seventeen she married a fisherman at Dungeness whose mother's maiden name was Serene Tart.

Photographer, David Smith

Sylvia Oiller, born in 1938, came from a farming background in nearby Lydd marrying into the Oiller family in 1955, her husband being a distant relative of Doris.

Photographer, David Smith

Two other important fishing families the Thomas' and the Richardsons' are represented by

Doreen Thomas born in New Cross, London in 1926
Photographer, David Smith

and **Marion Richardson** born in 1971.
Photographer, Ged Robinson

From Doris' memories spring an idyllic childhood at Dungeness in the 1930s; *"we had a wonderful childhood – we'd got all the open ground to play on – we got the sea. What more could you ask for."* Although times were financially hard her father was a good shot and supplemented their fish diet with wild rabbit and duck. The fishing families all owned their own milking goats that roamed freely on the Ness and the children's chores would be rounding up these goats or in Doris' case, collecting broom to light the fire. The shingle appeared to offer an area similar to common land and Doris can remember as many as forty children playing together, all from local families, on a place known as the *"battery"*. These did not include the children from *"the other end"*, whose fathers worked for the lighthouse or the Royal Naval Shore Signal Station, although they did all attend the same school on the beach, *"The School Beautiful"*:

"We'd got our own little school that we'd got to go to. That was about two mile away – we used to have to walk to school and take our dinner in a little satchel. There was about fifty or sixty in the school – two teachers – served as a little church as well. We learnt everything that there was to be learnt and we used to put on our own little plays at school and go back in the evenings for rehearsals."

A Performance by Pupils of The School Beautiful
Photograph courtesy of Doris Tart

The parents then would all trudge over the beach to the performance. In those days the road went no further than Derek Jarman's cottage and to walk over the shingle children and adults alike used *"baxters"* or more correctly *"backstays"*, a type of wooden flip-flop that fits over your shoe and functions like a snowshoe.

Dungeness School
Photograph courtesy of Doris Tart

The School Beautiful

Away by the sea where God's air blows free
Surrounded by beach and by stone
Stands a quaint little school
A school that we love and one we are proud to own
The school, the School Beautiful
The school we're proud to claim
The teachers ask through shine and shower
Always Play the Game – Play the Game.

Lillian B William (teacher at Dungeness during the 1920s)

Pauline Fair enjoyed a similar freedom as a child at Dungeness on arriving as a seven-year-old in 1950:

"I used to do a lot of walking out to the ponds out the back here. There's so much vegetation now, there wasn't so much then and there was these two crane ponds. I used to spend hours over there with a jam jar catching tiddlers, take my sandwiches over there and be over there all day, there was no fear, my mother never worried about me, you never saw a soul."

Railway Carriage Bungalow
Photographer, David Smith

As a newcomer Pauline found it difficult to integrate into the local community. She lived in one of the railway carriage bungalows that had begun to appear on the beach during the inter-war years. The land was then owned by Ashford Railway Works and as a privileged employee Pauline's father in 1946 had been allowed to purchase an old railway carriage. It was then transported to the beach by rail (the station had remained on the beach until the 'Beeching' cuts of 1963) and dragged across the shingle by a team of horses. These railway carriage bungalows nestled along the Point near the lighthouse and once converted were used as holiday and weekend homes. The travel writer Eric Newby describes staying in one for a holiday in the 1940s:

"Dungeness in December was out of this world all right. The wind howled over the shingle and among the dilapidated wooden buildings ... The inhabitants all seemed to have gone to earth for the winter. We found accommodation with suspicious ease in a disused railway carriage, at the extraordinary rental of four shillings a day."[1]

Pauline's father had been a keen angler and had initially used the railway carriage bungalow for weekends and holidays, but after four years of constantly travelling backwards and forwards to Dungeness they decided to move down permanently. They were one of the first families to make a permanent home in one of the railway carriage bungalows and she described how they were considered *"foreigners"*, the fishing families being the *"locals"*. The two communities *"never got on"*. The local school had closed in 1940 and the children from each community were transported to school in neighbouring Lydd in two separate taxis.

Even though her parents opened a small, busy teashop for anglers in their bungalow, Dungeness people found it very difficult to accept outsiders. *"Dad would have liked to get in with the lifeboat but they didn't want to know him."* Fishermen's 'cabons' or huts had been recorded at Dungeness as early as the mid-fourteenth century.[2] So it is not surprising that holiday home owners arriving

---

[1] Newby, Eric,. *Something Wholesale*. Picador 1985 (first published by Secker and Warburg 1962) pp181-182.
[2] Romney Marsh Research Trust, *A Seasonal Fishermen's Settlement at Dungeness, Kent.*, All Saint's Church Lydd, Parish Magazine, September 1998, p.13.

in the 1930s would be considered *"newcomers"*. Shepway District Council now recognises the distinct external differences between the fishermen's huts and the railway carriage bungalows in their conservation advice to property owners.[3] What this document fails to explain is how the fishermen's cabins and cottages with their net lofts and smokeries signified work whilst the railway carriage bungalows with their iconic verandas signified leisure. Only the residents of the beach themselves could appreciate the invisible line that divided the *"top enders"* from the *"bottom enders"*.

Fisherman's Cabin
Photographer, David Smith

---

[3] Shepway District Council. *Dungeness Conservation Area. Guidance to Property Owners.* (n.d.) circa 1994.

Although not 'local' Doreen, Sylvia and Marion did not encounter any sense of exclusion as they were immediately accepted through their marriage in to the fishing community. However, for Doreen aged 20 and newly married, arriving at Dungeness proved an unforgettable experience:

"The railway station was right across the beach there – you can't see it now – right over there it was – and I came down here – I worked in an office in London – I came down here in an off-white coat with leopard skin, a 'Mrs Minerver' hat stuck on the back of my head. Because he told me there wasn't much here you see. Which I understood – he didn't give me a false impression – but I was thinking of a kind of village at least and I stepped out on to the railway station and he said 'well there it is'."

Doreen saw herself as a distinct contrast to her mother-in law who *"used to walk about with a sort of a 'po' hat on and a shawl – all fishermen you see – and a black dress – all the things you imagine fishermen"* whilst she sported the fashionable Betty Grable hair style of the day, *"all curls on top"* and *"all blond because I blonded it"*.

Doreen also had to adjust to very different living conditions. Although she did not begin married life in the traditional fisherman's cottage but in the more conventional Royal Naval Shore Signal Station complex she still had no running water, gas or electricity. She adapted to using the same cooking facilities as the other fishermen's wives; a coal-fired range supplemented by a paraffin Primus stove and water had to be collected from a communal well. She recollected that the first time she cooked on a primus she set the wall alight. Her plea *"for a house with a toilet"* (her mother-in-law, like all the other fishermen's huts had an outside toilet *"with a wooden seat with a bucket underneath and they used to bury it in the beach"*), fortunately was met and proved a *"godsend"* even though it needed a bucket of water poured down it to flush.

Sylvia, on her marriage in 1955, lived next door to Doreen although by this time there was running water and electricity. She found Doreen extremely supportive (*"she mothered me"*). The children popped in to have breakfast with Doreen and Bill on the arrival of a new baby. Initially Sylvia had no knowledge of fishing other than liking *"smoked haddock and battered fish from the fish shop"*. She liked the life, but did find the lack of an expected routine difficult. Being dependent on the tides meant that *"with fishing you were all over the place"* and your husband *"came in plastered with scales"* so that *"you couldn't have people in for Sunday tea"*. She admitted, *"you miss the trees and primroses. My Mum sent me a tiny box of primroses in moss for my birthday every year"*. Pauline also hated Dungeness when she arrived from the countryside finding it *"too desolate, too windy and too cold"*. *"I always yearned for trees and green fields."*

For Pauline, Sylvia and Doreen, Dungeness provided their children with the same limitless freedom that Doris experienced as a child. Sylvia explained how *"They could just play in the bushes at the back here, they were quite safe"*. She had enjoyed taking breakfast down on the beach with them on fine summer mornings.

Marrying at the age of 19 into a family that had lived and fished at Dungeness since the 1800s, did not initially create any dramatic changes in Marion's life, as she continued with and completed her nursery nurse college training. Originating from Lewisham in London, Marion's family had moved to nearby St Mary's Bay over 30 years ago. With three small children, she still manages to help her husband selling fish from their shop that adjoins their house whilst also working two mornings a week at a local nursery school. By buying his grandfather's house her husband had retained the sense of continuity that has flowed through many of the fishermen's dwellings.

One of the older traditions in fishing is that women are not allowed on the boats - it's considered unlucky. Yet more recently Doreen's granddaughter had been fishing and Marion had been out with her husband, commenting that *"some girls do go afloat"*.

As the men worked a ten to twelve hour day with the time being dictated by the tides *"you didn't really see a lot of him. Really you brought up the children"*.(Doreen) Sylvia remembered a school essay written by one of her daughters that began: *"Sometimes my Dad goes herringing and then when he comes ashore he goes lug digging and then when he comes in he goes herringing."*

This work pattern meant that the women with young children were tied to the home. Physically getting out of Dungeness had been difficult for the older women, push chairs had to be dragged across the shingle, and losing the railway on the beach had further hampered mobility, although there were regular local buses and visiting tradesmen up until the late1960s. Doreen described the milkman arriving with two pails and a yolk also remembering that *"his milk was dreadful – he used to water it"* and Sylvia recollected a baker delivering twice a week, a butcher and a green grocer's van. Doris had memories from the 1930s of similar items being delivered by horse and cart and of Dungeness possessing its own post-office. At this time she very rarely travelled further than neighbouring Lydd, the greatest day of the year had been *"Lydd Club Day"* with its fair and carnival procession and they *"all had a new dress for that"*.

The physical remoteness of Dungeness, its isolation from any towns probably accentuated the feelings of a *"tight knit community"*. The women appreciated a combination of privacy and support as Doreen explained, *"Well, I suppose I have been here long enough. I know if I don't visit I could go to anyone's house and they'd help me. It's a community and there's nobody can interfere with me."* Somehow the open environment provides an open attitude allowing the women to be independent, to be accepted as themselves. Doreen laughingly commented, *"if I went out the back and danced naked they might think I was a bit mad but they'd say 'it's only Mrs Thomas'"*.

Against this sense of freedom has to be set the unifying hardships of fishing as a livelihood: *"If the fishing was bad and there was no money coming in everybody all helped one another."* (Doris) The women all agreed *"If you've got a lot of money one week and then the next week you got nothing - you don't just spend - you live the same regardless of what's coming in - might not go to sea for a month."* (Doreen) In spite of being younger, Marion also experiences this common bond: *"With the fishing you understand the other women friends, how that you don't always feel great – things aren't always going right on the boat and you know what they are worrying about."*

The weather too affects their livelihood. Boats cannot be launched from Dungeness in a strong easterly wind. Yet enforced leisure for the men does not automatically provide an opportunity for a family day out. Sylvia explained:

"Also the weather would govern your income which as well made it hard. When the weather was bad you couldn't really rejoice and take the kids out for an outing and spend money when you were not earning."

Fishing is also seasonal and *"if you had a bad herring season you had a bad Christmas."* (Doris) Pauline can remember her father-in-law excitedly clutching a five pound note exclaiming, *"we will be alright for Christmas!"* The collective memory of the older wives created a sense of community that faced and accepted a harsh reality: *"There was always hard times"* (Pauline) or *"A fisherman's life is a hard life"* (Doris) and *"Nothing in fishing is easy. Nothing."* (Doreen)

Even though the women remained on shore they supported their husbands in many ways, particularly assisting with the capstans on the launching or the heaving up of the boats. Although Sylvia had quite enjoyed helping with this Pauline expressed feelings of isolation in being left behind:

"So I'd go over, quite happy going over there and there was a lot of hullabaloo going on with them all getting afloat, you know, lots of shouting and lights flashing and everything and help them get afloat and pull the woods up after he'd gone which was hard work – especially if it was quite low tide up that steep bank – and then they'd all be gone and then I'd be left there – all on my own. And this would be about 4 o'clock in the morning – it was so dark and horrible – and I'd got to walk home on my own. It was horrible – I hated that bit."

The wives also helped in the preparation of fish to be sold or smoked from home. As Doris commented *"there isn't a fish I can't clean"* and Sylvia exclaimed *"the hours I've stood out with him in that shed every herring scraped by hand"*. Marion, being left handed found skinning the fish difficult but she has had *"to come to terms with people calling at all times"* and the shop being open every day in the summer until eight or nine o'clock in the evening. She now much prefers the winter (although *"not when I'm putting my hands in icy cold water to pick out his herrings that he's salting or pickling"*), as they can then close the shop at four o'clock, draw the curtains and be a family together. Laughingly Marion described how the older women had encouraged her to try shrimping (an occupation they all appeared to have enjoyed) but she had hated *"things round my legs in the sea"* much to the amusement of the other women.

As fishermen's wives they also had to face and accept the dangers of their husbands' occupation. For some it had become a part of a way of life, for others the fear always remained. The lifeboat represented an important focus for the community particularly as their husbands and sons formed the crew. In Marion's case as both her husband and father-in-law were crew members, neither were allowed out in the same boat together. She remembered a time when it had been *"really scarey"* waiting on the beach at night with the other women when her father-in-law as coxswain, had been called out to find two men lost at sea in a small boat. Yet, this did have its compensations, drawing the waiting women together and Marion explained how *"that makes you feel quite part of it all"* and *"you get to be involved with the other women and you make friends there"*.

Marion was too young to participate in the Women's Lifeboat Launchers team as this had ceased in the late 1970s with the introduction of a tractor to pull the boat over the shingle. Before this the launching was done manually, a task shouldered by the Dungeness fishermen's wives for the last hundred years. Doris, Sylvia and Pauline had all helped with this and Doris had been awarded a Gold badge for her services by the Royal National Lifeboat Institution as had Serena, Pauline's mother-in-law. The work involved laying heavy oak 'woods' or skids on to the shingle, usually in appalling weather conditions and at all times of the day and night, to enable the lifeboat to run into the sea. They had no specific clothes, just an official armband and their own wellingtons and mac.

Women Launchers – 1930s
Photograph courtesy of Doris Tart

Doris recounted the countless times she had been blown off the road on her bicycle and had to jump on again, peddling over to the lifeboat station in a gale. Contributing in this way not only eased their anxiety but strengthened the sense of continuity and community, with the same families consistently being represented by both the male crew and the women launchers.

This pattern is now changing. Whereas at one time the lifeboat crew consisted entirely of Tarts and Oillers, today there are no Oillers and only one Tart although there are still two Richardsons and one Thomas. It is the same with the fishermen's dwellings which, as the resident fishing community diminishes, are now being bought by *"outsiders"*. There were mixed reactions to this recent influx. Doris' experiences were that there were *"quite a lot of new folk – I think they'd look after you and speak to you. They must love Dungeness to come and live here"*. Others felt that Dungeness had undergone a process of *"Jarmanisation"* after the arrival of the film director, attracting artistic incomers. Marion humorously explained that:

"Derek used to help himself to things that he thought were old and useless to put in his garden and they would actually be very useful and people would get upset and say 'don't run off with that I need that for my winch!'"

However, that he had shared their deep affinity with the place had been appreciated. Sylvia, who had been a neighbour, commented on his book **derek jarman's garden**:

"He writes beautifully about Dungeness. I actually think if you'd loved Dungeness and you lay dying and someone read that to you, you'd be at Dungeness."

Dungeness, because of its lack of walls and boundaries exudes such a primeval essence of a wild open space we believe that it can belong to us all. Everywhere there is a sense of a freedom of spirit and lack of officialdom. The small self-built fishermen's huts, built as a *"squatters right"* long before the rigours of planning, are now an integral part of the landscape and like the indigenous plants, cling low to the shingle to escape the wind. Purpose built by the fishermen, the oldest house dates back to the 1860s and has withstood exposure to extremes of weather over the years. Yet, not only do these simple buildings offer the only shelter on this windswept beach, but they also provide much cared for attractive, comfortable homes.

These properties signify a visual map of inheritance for the fishing families. Their ownership can be traced back over the years through the collective memory of the community. Pauline felt that the gradual erosion of the community on the beach had contributed to the decline in the *"lovely atmosphere"* she had once so enjoyed.

She had been saddened by the loss of her husband's numerous and supportive relatives *"that were all close"* and had surrounded her during her early married life. There had been magical Christmases when a few of the fishermen would black their faces with cork and dress up in home-made coloured silk *"Andy Pandy type suits with black fluffy buttons. They'd have little hats and they'd put red lipstick on. My father-in-law would play the drums, Charlie Richardson played the bones – Johnny Oiller was very musical – he played the piano accordion."* They would go from house to house and play and be given a drink until *"by the time they got to The Pilot they would be absolutely blotto"*. Then there would be a tug o' war competition between the men and women followed by a football match between the same sides. Yet interestingly Marion, representing a new generation of fishermen's wives, had firmly stated *"When its Christmas I like it best"*. She had enjoyed the resurrection of the tug o' war and the football match where there were *"lots and lots of people of mixed ages"*, all of whom were family and friends. Her fondest memories were of spending Christmas Day visiting the numerous older family members still living on the beach.

Marion's enthusiasm and sense of privilege in belonging to this extended family that has lived and fished at Dungeness for so many years signifies the existence of a vibrant community today. That the original fishing community has survived, that so many memories have been retained, all enable us to appreciate how Dungeness originally belonged solely to the fisher folk. The necessity now is to ensure that this unique history is recorded so that all of us that are attracted to the bleak wildness of Dungeness can not only appreciate the past but also understand the present.

*****

The income from fishing was always unpredictable and when the wages were at their best, the men's hours were long and awkward. Always they had to keep some money by for the leaner times.

When the Little Billy first came home to Dungeness beach she was the most powerful vessel there. She had a six horsepower engine, while most of the others had only three and a half horsepower. These boats were used in spring for trawling out in Rye Bay, in autumn for mackerel drifting and in the winter for drift netting for sprats and herring.

In autumn they would go out into the shipping lanes, lay out about 800 yards of mackerel drift net, just as the sun was sinking, and hope that their judgement had been right for where the shoals of mackerel would rise and swim as it got dark. If a ship bore down on the nets, they would frantically wave a paraffin soaked flare and hope that the ship's helmsman would know what the meaning was.

About the third week in October the herring nets would be brought down from the net lofts, the nets would be laced together and the floats of "bobbers" attached ready for the season.

If the herring shoals did not arrive in any quantity and the weather was better for sprat fishing, then the sprat nets would be got ready. I can remember standing by the boats waiting for the signs that the sprats were shoaling. The seagulls would pick up sprats from the top of the water and if there were very large shoals there was a change in the colour of the sea.

In 1946 I left Lydd school to join my father and elder brother fishing for a living from Dungeness. Although I was used to the boats and had a few short trips under my belt, it came as a great shock to be called from my bed at 3.30 am on the first morning of employment as a young fisherman. We went trawling in the Little Billy and as we rounded the point and headed Southwest into Rye Bay, I remember standing next to my father who was at the tiller.

Because of the small engine we could only tow the trawl in the direction that the tide was flowing. So, if we left the beach on the ebb tide, we would steam about an hour to the fishing grounds. Then we would put the trawl down and tow it to the westward for about one and a half hours. Then, after retrieving the trawl by hand, we would have to go back eastwards for about an hour. While we were travelling we would be sorting out the fish we had caught from the rubbish and small fry, gutting them and getting ready for the next pull with the trawl. By the time we had completed the next pull, the tide would be on the change and we would be able to tow back towards Dungeness Point again. Most days we were able to fit four pulls of the trawl in a day's fishing, returning to the beach by about 3.00 pm. By the time we had heaved the boat up on to its station, unloaded that catch and made ready for the next trip we had worked a fourteen-hour day.

Ken Oiller

Artists at Dungeness – Keith Clements

To the visual artist, Dungeness is itself a virtual abstraction, meeting the painter, sculptor and photographer more than halfway. The stark, dark silhouettes of unplanned but interrelated cottages and bungalows, the adapted railway carriages, old boats and sheds, the fishing boats, beached between the detritus of rotting timbers, rope, rusting metal and wire are all set against the dramatic width of a seemingly ever changing sea and sky. Few have responded substantially to this abundance of material.

The technical drawings of the successive lighthouses at Dungeness Point, from the first tower of 1792 onwards, are of historic rather than aesthetic interest.

Probably the first noteworthy artists to work in the area during the 1880s and 1890s were the marine watercolourist TB Hardy, Frank Brangwyn who made some of his earliest seascapes here and the modest painter and etcher, Frank Short who worked directly on to the plate from life.

It was not until after the First World War that any major artists were attracted to the area. Paul Nash (1889-1946) came to Kent in the 1920s. He had seen active service in the Artists' Rifles at Ypres and after injury and convalescence returned to the Front as an official War Artist. The discreet charm and the peace and quiet of this often eerie place must have been an antidote to the horrors of war. Living first in a tiny cottage overshadowed by the sea wall at Dymchurch and, in 1923, moving to a larger house, Pantile Cottage (now demolished) on the road to Lydd, Nash drew, painted and photographed some of his most memorable images. One of the masterpieces deriving from this period, **Nostalgic Landscape**, is dated 1923-38, during which time he had moved to Iden, in the

Nostalgic Landscape – Paul Nash 1923-38
©Tate Gallery

Rother Valley, spent four years in Rye and, in 1933, moved to Avebury in Wiltshire.

In all of Nash's pictures begun or realised at Dymchurch, Dungeness is merely a backdrop to the seawall, the breakwaters and the waves. Whilst he always retains a strong sense of place and the origins and elements are still clearly recognisable, at his best he transcends the setting: **Nostalgic Landscape** – the title itself is generalised – has affinities with the artist's ongoing connections and preoccupations, with abstraction and, of course, surrealism. The picture is an amalgam of feelings and influences as well as the summation of Nash's experience of war and peace, of life and art in relation to the place itself. When he reworked this seminal painting, eventually away from the subject, it is as though distance had lent enchantment and the picture has become more about time, space and memory.

John Piper (1903-1992) seemed to paint everywhere – particularly in Britain and extensively in France and parts of Italy. Probably through his older friend Paul Nash, he first came to Dungeness around 1936. Painter, printmaker, illustrator, ceramicist, stained glass and theatre designer and writer, Piper was a prolific all rounder in the arts. He too, as a young man in the 1930s, became caught up with abstraction, but his innate instincts were always more towards the romantic, to expressionism and to landscape in general. *'Dungeness and Newhaven, ships and lighthouses are continuing Piper themes'*, wrote Richard Ingrams and quoted the artist in **Piper's Places:**

'The Lighthouse, the lifeboat house with its slip way, the Customs house, the boat building shed are all functional buildings, but the builders of them never thought of attempting to banish personal taste. They are functional but they are something else as well. They have strength, gaiety of design and colour (even if it is only

the gaiety of black and white) and they are usually in startling contrast with their surroundings.'[1]

In 1936, Piper made a number of drawings, paintings and collages of the Dungeness lighthouse and views of the bay from Littlestone. These were not compositionally dissimilar to those by Nash from Dymchurch, but temperamentally and technically more spontaneous and far less stylised.

Piper returned in 1947 after the Second World War when he was commissioned to write and illustrate a guide to the Romney Marsh.

'Once again Piper was back to one of his earliest loves – the neglected seashore. He ignored the more picturesque Martello towers of Hythe and the Dymchurch Wall and returned instead to Dungeness, the wilderness of shingle ...... which he had once compared to an oversized nursery floor littered with coastguard cottages, huts, stones, lighthouses and flagpoles.' [2]

Dungeness, Kent (1947) looks toward the lighthouse from the west. The sea is lapping the shore on the right, the sky possibly near to imploding but with its touch of blue, less threatening than the famously thunderous Piper skies. The textural effects are delivered with a delicious abandon and are typically theatrical beyond the actual size of the picture – a mere 6 inches by 8 inches yet the picture evokes a remarkable feeling of place.

Eric Ravilious (1903-42) was born in Eastbourne and studied at the Royal College of Art under Paul Nash. In 1940, he had been appointed an official war artist and worked his way along the south coast from Newhaven to Dover, painting the sea defences. His

---

[1] Ingrams, Richard and Piper, John, *Piper's Places*, Chatto & Windus/The Hogarth Press London 1983 p25
[2] as above p118

Dungeness, Kent – John Piper, 1947
Reproduced by kind permission of the Piper Estate

Dungeness Lighthouse – Eric Ravilious, 1940
© Estate of Eric Ravilious, All Rights reserved, DACS 1999

dynamic composition of the **Dungeness Lighthouse** whilst intensely personal and recognisably Ravilious, stylistically owes something to the influence of Nash and his Dymchurch essays of the 1930s.

After Piper, it was some forty years before another major figure appeared on the Dungeness scene: *'John Owen painted the people of the fishing community at Dungeness during the mid-1960s ...Charles N Longbotham explored the bleak atmosphere of the coast in winter studies in watercolour in 1967. Dennis Hanceri, in his favourite medium of watercolour and body colour painted Thames barges off Dungeness in the mid-1970s, giving a sensation of the misty distances typical of this part of the coast. Eileen James, a self-taught artist ... Painted the fishing vessels and their crews on the foreshore here in the late 1970s.'* [3]

It was Derek Jarman (1942-94) who really put Dungeness on the cultural map, nationally, even internationally. His arrival aroused both curiosity and concern among the locals whose families had lived there undisturbed for several generations. In 1987 he bought Prospect Cottage in the shadow of the Nuclear Power Station, to live in their midst. This wacky, extrovert, multi-media, high profile artist certainly brought fame and a whiff of notoriety to a forgotten corner of England. From student days he had always been newsworthy, as much for his art as for his life-style: Jarman was, unashamedly, conspicuously gay and also a prominent campaigner for gay rights and against censorship.

Jarman's life and art have been extensively documented and analysed in detail elsewhere. What is of concern and relevance here is the influence of the place on Jarman; and, conversely, his influence on Dungeness.

---

[3] Hemming, Charles, *British Painters of the Coast and Sea, A History and Gazetteer*, Victor Gollancz, London 1988, p128

Trained in fine art as a painter, Jarman worked early on in the theatre as a stage designer, gravitating towards film, designing sets, initially for the notoriously flamboyant director Ken Russell. It is surprising that some of Russell's facility in cutting film seemed not to rub off on Jarman. Derek Thomson, the film critic and historian, said of Jarman that his *'hysterical inventiveness, his camaraderie, his serene anger – all these things need the condition of confinement. The films may also need an audience of inmates. In other words, he has a habit of alienating and scorning those on the other side of the bars.'* [4]

Before the move to Dungeness, Jarman's paintings often seemed unexceptional essays in composition, pigment and texture. One of his first influences was Paul Nash, particularly the geometric and surreal aspects. However, the new environment began to impress and intrigue him and, by the early 90s, he started using bitumen or tar to bind some of the objects found thrown up by the sea, literally reflecting the actual experience of place and the volatile coastal weather.

In 1986, Jarman was diagnosed HIV positive. From then on, although he continued to work in a wide range of media and to actively support the causes for which he had become well known, his health steadily deteriorated resulting in a gradual loss of sight. Despite this, his best work must be from this last period when he was most physically fragile but intellectually sensitive.

The Garden was his swansong and his most accessible work: a film; a book of exquisite poetry and prose; passionate paintings and sculptures relate to the experience of cultivating, against all odds, the shingle surrounding Prospect Cottage and above all the garden itself, which has become a shrine to the artist and a unique tourist

---

[4] Thomson, David, *A Biographical Dictionary of Film*, Andre Deutsch, London 1994, p372

attraction. Amongst the flora and fauna, and flotsam and jetsam of Dungeness fellow artists, historians, ecologists, horticulturists and visitors can all respond to and identify with some part of this gentle, sad but joyful celebration of Jarman's last years

Unlike so much of his more obscure, art-house output, in **The Garden**, Jarman achieved what he might have wanted all along. Through a primitive directness and fundamental simplicity, he managed to create a contemplative, democratic and egalitarian work of art that, without any pretensions, marries east and west, north and south and communicates with everyone. Hence, perhaps, its continuing popularity.

Of the artists associated with Dungeness, certainly the most consistently involved and the one whose work is most conspicuously reflective of the place, is Brian Yale (1936-). In 1979, some years before Jarman's arrival he and his wife Sheila, an artist and designer working mostly with fabrics and textiles, bought Ness Cottage, next to Prospect Cottage. Since the late 60s, Yale had painted in and around the sea and the coastal strip of Dungeness and the Romney Marsh but as he says, '*It is not a picturesque landscape, it is an atmosphere, a large flat area illuminated like no other place in England, where the sea is supreme.*' [5]

Yale has lectured at art colleges in London and the United States and was for twenty years an environmental artist and designer with the Architects' Department of the late Greater London Council. He has a wide-ranging interest in poetry and music, in the environment and ecology, in design and the arts generally. He sees no distinctions between painting and sculpture, or between fine and applied art and continues to work using a variety of mixed media.

---

[5] Yale, Brian, *Dungeness: Landscapes on the Edge*, Wolseley Fine Arts, London 1996

'Landscape has always been a primary source of inspiration', he says.

Soon after acquiring Ness Cottage, Yale too made sculptures in the garden and began to cultivate the shingle, doubtless later inspiring his neighbour Derek Jarman at Prospect Cottage. *'I could stand on the doorstep of my cottage at Dungeness and in one day paint the sunrise and sunset, storms at sea, Constable clouds, great ships, people, fog and wind, and all this without moving a jot. It is the sea which holds my attention...the vastness and movement stirs something in us, perhaps it is the realisation that finally we are just passing by.'* [6]

Spirit of the Air – Brian Yale, 1990
Reproduced by kind permission of Brian Yale

---

[6] Yale, Brian, *Dungeness: Landscapes on the Edge*, Wolseley Fine Arts, London 1996

Off the Beach – Brian Yale, 1993
Reproduced by kind permission of Brian Yale

There is surely a natural connection between Brian Yale's adoption of Dungeness and his continuing preoccupation with the First World War battlefields in France. The theme is innately melancholy but his canvases, underlined with telling quotations on the foot of each frame, have a moving optimism reminiscent of Paul Nash's masterpiece of 1918, **We are making a new world**.

Yale has said that his intentions and hopes are always to avoid both the obviously prettier aspects of the seaside and the more hackneyed arrangements of the elements. In **Spirits of the Air** of 1990, he has caught an unusual moment when a film crew landed an aircraft on the shingle near the lighthouse; and, in a mixed media construction of 1993, **Off the Beach,** he integrates the materials scavenged from the shore into the actual subject itself.

'I work on the spot, or from memory, or drawings and photographs, much depends on the subject and interpretation ... I am trying to encapsulate in a single image, the awesomeness of ordinary things.' [7]

In his transformations of the ordinary and his persistent pursuit of the scope and the minutiae of Dungeness, Yale has made the place firmly his own. In this he seems to echo something of TS Eliot's lines of 1932

> *"...time is always time*
> *And place is always and only place*
> *And what is natural is actual only for one time*
> *And only for one place."*

*****

---

[7] Yale, Brian, *Dungeness: Landscapes on the Edge*, Wolseley Fine Arts, London 1996

At first the war did not mean much to me as a seven-year-old, but we were soon to see some great changes to our lives at Dungeness.

The army arrived and took over our small school as living accommodation. Six-inch guns were installed in an old First World War fortress that stood nearly at the end of Dungeness Point. Gradually more military personnel appeared and set up roadblocks on the road from Lydd.

My father joined the Royal Observer Corps, which was formed to warn of approaching enemy aircraft and keep a look out for any suspicious vessels that might be moving along the channel.

Early in the war the MV Roseburn was torpedoed just off Dungeness Point. My father was on duty in the watchtower and saw two German E Boats (fast torpedo launches) each with a single light bearing down on the Roseburn. He called HQ, but as it was so early in the war no one believed him. He said, "If you listen you will hear the explosions", and sure enough a few minutes later there were two large explosions as the torpedoes struck.

As the German army advanced across France, Dungeness became a restricted zone. Everyone entering the area was stopped at a checkpoint and had to produce a special pass to be allowed in. Soon there were minefields and a long stretch of the coastline was fortified by arranging a structure of scaffolding poles designed to delay any enemy tanks.

The fishermen were now only allowed to go out on the beach in daylight hours. Many of them joined the local Home Guard unit and the boats were armed (in a fashion) each vessel being issued with a .303 rifle and two of the fleet with a Bren gun.

I remember one day when the local fleet were all drift fishing for herring and a Dornier bomber cut across the bay and fired on the boats. They returned the fire with their small arms and the German bomber released a bomb, which fortunately missed, before turning back towards the French coast. Listening to the radio the next day we heard that Lord Haw-Haw had claimed that the British fishing fleet had been completely destroyed off Dungeness that day!

Memories of the war years include the sight of a Spitfire struggling back to base with half of one wing shot away; a Junkers 88 flying along the beach with a white scarf fluttering from the window before crash landing in front of the Britannia pub - the crew surrendered; three German fighter planes chasing a Spitfire along the coast towards Hythe. The pilot of the Spitfire purposefully drew the fighters on to the batteries of anti-aircraft guns.

Then there were the DoodleBugs. When they came over we would stand in the porch of our cottage and watch as at first the ships in the bay and then the guns on the beach would open fire. It was always a bit of fun for us children to watch the different ways these flying bombs would crash when they were hit.

During the later stages of the war when the British troops had landed in Normandy and were pushing ever further into France, PLUTO – Pipeline Under The Ocean – was launched out from Dungeness. Many of the bungalows were taken over and pumping stations were set up in them. The pipes were buried in the beach and from there they were laid across the Channel from a specially designed vessel.

One of these pipes actually went across the front of our cottage, within about two feet of the front door step. One autumn evening an army officer came banging at the door shouting "put all the lamps out, quick as you can!" When we looked out we could see why he was so agitated. A great stream of petrol was squirting into the air just a few feet away. Luckily we had no fires burning.

The next morning when we went to pump water we realised that all the underground streams had been contaminated. The military provided us with bowsers and soon a permanent water supply was installed to all the cottages.

Ken Oiller

Conservation and Wildlife – Simon Busuttil

The wild, strange landscape of Dungeness is the result of the interaction of natural and human forces and the last 60 years have been a period of unprecedented change. Whether there has been a net gain or loss of landscape or wildlife is very much a question of value even when we approach this question using scientific concepts such as biodiversity.

The area was first recognised in print for its ornithological importance in 1824. Early in the twentieth century the Royal Society for the Protection of Birds (RSPB) began paying "watchers" to look after the seabirds that nested on the shingle and around the few areas of open water that existed then.

In 1929 the RSPB acquired its first landholding on the 'ness. When it sold the reserve at Cheyne Court on Romney Marsh early in the 1930s Dungeness became the Society's oldest reserve thus ensuring its right to a special place within the RSPB's history.

The interaction between men and the landscape at this time was already reflecting the changes to come later in the century. Pressure on the natural resources of the place was increased through the collection of eggs and specimens for natural history collections. Not only could collectors travel down from London but they could also pay local people to collect their specimens. It was to stop this that the first watchers were appointed. This kind of recreational pressure is a problem that still exists for those charged with the protection of the area – today, in the 1990s, increasing numbers of visitors and four-wheel drive and off-road vehicles pose a new threat.

Early this century the need to preserve areas of land of importance for scientific, cultural, landscape or wildlife reasons was just being recognised. Dungeness appeared on the earliest of these lists produced in 1915 by the Society for the Promotion of Nature Reserves.

The culmination of this process was to have been the declaration of a National Nature Reserve (NNR) across the area. However, the loss of the public enquiry in 1958 against the building of the first nuclear power station at Dungeness and the subsequent withdrawal from the NNR process, left the area even more exposed to a growing economic force: the requirement for aggregates for the construction industries and the expanding motorway programme.

In 1951 the government went some way to recognising the ecological value of the 'ness by notifying it as a Site of Special Scientific Interest (SSSI). However, it was only in 1998 that the long waited for NNR was finally declared.

The acquisition of large areas of the 'ness by the RSPB has been made possible by the mandate and financial support of its million members. This has held in check the damaging economic development that would have otherwise destroyed the 'ness and perhaps left little of value to conserve by the millennium.

View of the RSPB Reserve towards the Power Station
Photograph courtesy of the RSPB

Dungeness is a place where migrant birds can be seen seeking cover and food in the scrub or soaring overhead en route to breeding or wintering grounds elsewhere in the world – a special place in the annals of birdwatching.

Shingle has been extracted from Dungeness for over 100 years. In the latter half of the last century it was dug by hand and no areas of open water were created. Since the 1920s, the ability to dig below the water level on the 'ness has existed. With economic and technological development accelerating after 1945, increased areas of open water have been created as the aggregates industry has been able to dig larger and deeper holes using draglines, floating barges and huge suction pumps. Through this use of the land the relationship between conservation and industry evolved into a surprising new opportunity for wildlife on the 'ness.

Areas of open water, the by-product of this industrial process, are probably the longest lasting impact on the landscape and ecology of Dungeness. Long after the power stations have been dismantled, this new land of lakes will continue to be a place rich in birds and other wildlife.

A huge aquifer of fresh unpolluted water lies below the shingle and has also been exploited since the end of the nineteenth century. Up to two million gallons per day are extracted by the Folkestone and Dover Water Company to provide drinking water for the growing towns to the east. Hidden for hundreds of years beneath the shingle, the exposure of areas of open water by the gravel industry has created a habitat that was previously rare on the shingle. The wildlife that has reacted by colonising this new habitat is equally rare, adding to the rich biodiversity of Dungeness.

When viewed from this perspective, the real value to wildlife conservation of gravel extraction is revealed more clearly. It is a temporary activity, the end result of which, if carefully planned and managed, has the potential to replace some of the vast areas of natural and semi-natural habitats that have been lost through agricultural intensification, industrial and infrastructural expansion in the last thirty years.

The seabirds that the first watchers had looked after disappeared during the war. The army needed to practise and Dungeness made an ideal site. The soldiers brought canteens and edible rubbish which led to an increase in the number of foxes, which remain to this day. Increased disturbance of their eggs and young by the foxes led to the seabirds' extinction. In the 1970s the RSPB encouraged one gravel company - ARC - to leave shingle islands in a gravel pit that was being dug within the RSPB reserve. Seabirds returned to breed on these islands, able to nest safe from the foxes. It was the first step in turning around the decline of the wildlife at Dungeness.

Fragmentation of the landscape by roads, pylons and gravel pits and the increase in fox numbers and disturbance also led to the extinction, in 1968, of the stone curlew whose evocative, haunting nocturnal whistle was one of the characteristic sounds of the 'ness. The Kentish plovers that had once nested had gone by 1931, their nesting sites destroyed by housebuilding and the construction of the light railway.

Nature changes all the time. New birds colonised – Mediterranean gulls nested for the first time in Britain at Dungeness in 1981 and a colony of Sandwich terns returned to breed in Kent - the county in which they were originally named – on the seabird islands in 1978.

The little ringed plover, a close relative of the lost Kentish plover, colonised the changed habitat. Arriving each March from Africa they join other ground nesting birds – ringed plovers and oystercatchers within the sanctuary of the expanding reserve.

In the 1980s the public's perception of nature as something scarce and therefore to be valued strengthened and membership of charities such as the RSPB increased. Equally, the gravel industry's need to meet the demands of public and planners forced them to make greater concessions to the demands of those determined not to see this opportunity to create new habitats squandered.

The new gravel pits were designed with their future as a conservation resource specifically in mind. Careful planning and management have created a mosaic of habitats, which, in a small way, replace some of the wetlands that have been destroyed in the last 30 years.

The populations of waterbirds both breeding and arriving from northern and eastern Europe to spend the winter on the developing wetland have grown enormously in the past decade. In 1970 maybe just 100 widgeon – a handsome duck from northern Europe – wintered in the area. In 1997 almost 10,000 did. Their call is a whistle that can be heard day and night during the winter from the fields and lakes at the edge of the shingle where the stone curlew once called during the summer.

Since the largest gathering ever of world leaders at the Earth Summit at Rio in 1992, biodiversity has been the concept at the centre of the thinking of much of the conservation movement. Biodiversity simply means the variety of life around us from the microscopic bacteria to the tallest trees, encompassing all wildlife both common and rare. It is about what exists not just in the tropical rainforest but at a local level, on our own doorstep on the 'ness!

So in the 1990s it is the awareness of the non-bird interest of Dungeness that has changed our perception of what is important here. Even without any birds this place is worth protecting.

One third of all the plant species in Britain are found here – over 600 species. Several of these are incredibly rare – the stinking hawksbeard is found only on the 'ness in Britain. It was extinct in the wild. Seeds from Dungeness were held at Kew and provided the stock for a reintroduction programme. In 1996 Jersey cudweed was discovered growing on the RSPB reserve - its spread over the next few years has been monitored closely and there are now more plants on the artificially created silt banks than there are in the rest of Britain.

Cladonia Lichen – one of the several species present at Dungeness
Photograph courtesy of the RSPB

And the 'ness is the third most important site in Britain for invertebrates. There is even a species that is endemic to Dungeness – a leafhopper *Aphrodes Duffieldi* – that is found nowhere else in the world. Three rare damp-sand loving beetles colonised the unsaleable silt washed out of the shingle and used to edge the new pits. The wonderful sounding *Omophron limbatum, Dyschirius obscurus* and *Heterocerus hispidus* are still only found in the Dungeness area in Britain.

The globally threatened medicinal leech thrives in the old gravel workings feeding on amphibians, fish and birds. Once collected by the million by peasants in the eighteenth century throughout Europe to supply the medical profession this species has disappeared from much of its range because of pollution, over-collecting and habitat destruction. There are more in the gravel pits around Dungeness than the rest of Britain put together.

Medicinal Leech – more live in the pits at Dungeness than anywhere else in Britain
Photograph courtesy of the RSPB

This is the nearest thing we have to a desert in Britain – stony, free draining with almost no soil. A lack of nutrients holds the vegetation back to an early stage of succession – sparse and specialised. The stones heat up quickly during the day and give up their heat slowly at night, hot in summer, cold in winter – not a place where nothing lives but a place where specialists thrive.

Nottingham Catchfly – a typical plant of the undisturbed vegetated shingle
Photograph courtesy of the RSPB

This is the paradox of Dungeness. The shingle vegetation and invertebrate communities are internationally recognised as of value and protected accordingly. The several industries, including the gravel industry, have destroyed hundreds of acres of this unique habitat.

But what has been created by the aggregates industry, at first by accident and later by design is increasingly being recognised as being of value in its own right. It could be argued that it would have been better if the gravel industry had never dug a single pit at Dungeness but equally it can be argued that biodiversity at Dungeness has increased as a result of this activity.

The big questions for conservationists are how can we protect our dwindling wildlife resources? How many reserves should there be and how big should they be? Do we really want to see our rich and varied places remain only as ghettos in reserves? If not, how do we conserve wildlife in the wider countryside?

The questions are relevant to Dungeness. It is such a unique place that it is internationally important for biodiversity. But, people also live and work here, others visit. Creative solutions will be needed to conserve the best of the 'ness whilst allowing it to continue to be a place for the people who use it and those who love it.

Conservation is not about the past but the future. It is not a matter of just preserving what there is but of being creative, seizing opportunities and taking risks. At Dungeness, how much water can be abstracted from the aquifer without irreparably damaging the wildlife interest? What do we do when the nuclear power stations are decommissioned? Do we as a society continue the unsustainable task of attempting to hold this mobile mass of shingle static or do we allow longshore drift to again pull the 'ness eastwards? How far will we go to protect the biodiversity of the place? Conservation will play a central part in the value that we place upon Dungeness.

*****

I have always thought that I was privileged to have been born at Dungeness. There have been many changes over the years. Now only four of the original fishing families live within the boundaries of the Dungeness estate. Some of the younger fishermen have moved to more conventional housing and the fleet has been joined by fishermen from elsewhere.

People who come to visit either love it or hate it. Many who have come here for a short spell have returned to inhabit one of the small holiday chalets near the lighthouse, or have moved into one of the fishermen's bungalows as they have been vacated and come on to the market.

I am optimistic that in the future the outward appearance of Dungeness will change very little. Now that it is a National Nature Reserve I feel sure that the people who visit will enjoy and respect the area and all that it has to offer.

Ken Oiller aged 4
Photograph courtesy of Ken Oiller

Dungeness is a unique place. Of that there is no doubt. I have lived here all of the sixty-five years of my life and I have some wonderful memories of this unique shingle bank that juts out into the English Channel.

Ken Oiller

The Contributors

This book has been written by a group of people linked by a common interest in and fascination with Dungeness. Drawn together, each has contributed according to their particular area of interest and expertise. The memories of Ken Oiller surround the other contributions.

Simon Busuttil is the RSPB Dungeness Area Manager. He has been working in conservation for 11 years of which 8 have been with the RSPB. He lives on the RSPB reserve at Dungeness and is fully committed to the conservation of the area.

Keith Clements is a painter, writer, lecturer and illustrator. He is a concerned environmentalist and has a love of the area, which he has known for all of his life. Dungeness has had particular impact on artists over the years, and Keith has written about their work here.

Sue Davies was introduced to Dungeness through her work in editing this book. The fascination of the place and its inhabitants together with the commitment of the contributors has made it a most enjoyable project.

Mariana Hollis first came to know Dungeness and to admire its strange beauty when she was a student of landscape ecology at Wye College. The individualistic scenery and specialised vegetation made the area a mecca for landscape students. She is a landscape architect, historian and lecturer and has written conservation and management studies of other waterside and coastal locations.

Ken Oiller has lived at Dungeness all his life. Having retired from fishing he has been a local councillor since 1995. He finds the work both interesting and frustrating but perseveres in his commitment to the future of the area and Dungeness in particular.

Ged Robinson, who is the inspiration and energy behind this book, first visited Dungeness to research the history of the fisherman's huts and the railway carriage bungalows. She believes that the only way to understand Dungeness is to look at the whole area holistically and spatially and at a national rather than a local level. Because of the important organisations and issues represented at Dungeness the local fishing community is in danger of being permanently eclipsed. We have been privileged to gain an insight into the lives of those stalwart families that have lived and fished at Dungeness over the last few centuries.

David Smith is a photographer based in Brighton. He has always been interested in landscape and relished the opportunity of working in the unique landscape of Dungeness. Other recent commissions of local interest include a look at the visual impact of the Channel Tunnel on the Borough of Ashford.

Ginny Smith has always been fascinated by the windswept marshes that lie between Rye and New Romney, in Kent. A visit to a friend's wooden cottage, created from a railway carriage on Dungeness, introduced her to the unique environment of the gravel spit and the people who live there. Professionally she works with groups on their interactions with one another and their environment. Dungeness presented an opportunity to understand the impact of the great bulk of the nuclear power stations on the community who have lived and worked in their shadow for many years.

Acknowledgements

We would like to thank the staff and volunteers who have over many years helped to protect the best of Dungeness through their work on the RSPB nature reserve.

The artist Brian Yale and the interviewees: Doris Tart, Doreen Thomas, Sylvia Oiller, Pauline Fair and Marion Richardson.

*****

We are very aware that there is much more of interest in, around and about Dungeness – the Light Railway, the lighthouse, and the pubs to mention just a few topics. These pages have scratched the surface and revealed a little of the history, memories and creativity originating from Dungeness. There will be more.

Bibliography

Carpenter, Edward, *Dungeness Lighthouses*, Margaret F Bird & Associates, Lydd, Kent 1996, 1998

Clements, Keith, *Paul Nash, Dymchurch and the Romney Marsh*, Artists and Places, 'The Artist' April 1986

Constable, Freda, *The England of Eric Ravilious*, Scolar Press, London 1982

Hemming, Charles, *British Painters of the Coast and Sea*, A History and Gazetteer, Victor Gollancz, London 1988

Ingrams, Richard and Piper, John, *Piper's Places*, Chatto & Windus/The Hogarth Press, London 1983

derek jarman's garden, Thames & Hudson, London 1995

Derek Jarman: A Portrait, Thames & Hudson, London 1996

Nash, Margaret, (ed. Paul Nash), *Fertile Image*, Faber & Faber, London 1951, 1975

Newby, Eric, *Something Wholesale*, Picador 1985, Secker and Warburg 1962

Read, Herbert, *Paul Nash*, Penguin Modern Painters, Harmondsworth, Middlesex 1949

Romney Marsh Research Trust, *A Seasonal Fisherman's Settlement at Dungeness, Kent*, All Saint's Church, Lydd, Parish Magazine, September 1998

Shepway District Council, *Dungeness Conservation Area, Guidance to Property Owners* (n.d.) c. 1994

Thomson, David, *A Biographical Dictionary of Film*, Andre Deutsch, London 1994

Yale, Brian, *Variations on Life*, Llantarnam Grange Art Centre, Cwmbran, Gwent 1993

Yale, Brian, *Dungeness: Landscapes on the Edge*, Wolseley Fine Arts, London 1996

Yorke, Malcolm, *The Spirit of Place*, Constable, London 1988

Distributed by Sutton House, Iford, East Sussex, BN7 3EU
01273 476847